THE HERMIT'S KISS

ALSO BY RICHARD TELEKY

FICTION

Winter in Hollywood
Pack Up the Moon
The Paris Years of Rosie Kamin
Goodnight, Sweetheart and Other Stories

NON-FICTION

Hungarian Rhapsodies: Essays on Ethnicity, Identity and Culture

ANTHOLOGY

The Oxford Book of French-Canadian Short Stories
(with Marie-Claire Blais)

THE HERMIT'S KISS

Richard Teleky

Fitzhenry & Whiteside

The Hermit's Kiss Copyright © 2006 Richard Teleky

Fitzhenry and Whiteside Limited
195 Allstate Parkway, Markham, Ontario L3R 4T8

In the United States:
311 Washington Street, Brighton, Massachusetts 02135

www.fitzhenry.ca godwit@fitzhenry.ca

Fitzhenry & Whiteside acknowledges with thanks the Canada Council for the Arts, and the Ontario Arts Council for their support of our publishing program. We acknowledge the financial support of the Government of Canada through the Book Publishing Industry Development Program (BPIDP) for our publishing activities.

ONTARIO ARTS COUNCIL
CONSEIL DES ARTS DE L'ONTARIO

Canada Council   Conseil des Arts
for the Arts   du Canada

Library and Archives Canada Cataloguing in Publication
Teleky, Richard, 1946-
The hermit's kiss / Richard Teleky.
Poems.
ISBN 1-55041-571-9
I. Title.
PS8589.E375H47 2006   C811'.54   C2006-900357-2

U.S. Publisher Cataloging-in-Publication Data (Library of Congress Standards)
Teleky, Richard, 1946-
The hermit's kiss / Richard Teleky.
[112] p. : col. ill. ; cm.
Summary: Poems explore the themes of sickness and suffering, age and loneliness,
and abandon the local in favor of the literary.
ISBN 1-55041-571-9 (pbk.)
1. Canadian poetry – 21st century. I. Title.
811.54 dc22 PR9199.3.T417H47 2006

Cover and interior design by
Karen Thomas Petherick, Intuitive Design International

Cover photograph (Budapest stairwell)
by Richard Teleky

This ancient forest friendly book contains 100% post consumer, recycled material.
Printed and bound in Canada

1 3 5 7 9 10 8 6 4 2

For Penelope Tzougros

CONTENTS

I

II

III

IV

V

VI

THE HERMIT'S KISS

I

"That day – a fine early autumn day – Sindbad dressed as carefully as befitted a man over three hundred years old. He selected a light-colored tie and brightly polished shoes."

– Gyula Krúdy, *The Adventures of Sindbad*

RE-READING *ANNA KARENINA*

i.

> Beyond Garbo,
with a detour past
Vivien Leigh and other
moody types who've
played her for PBS like a
Manchester matron, past,
even, Sophie Marceau and
her pert little nose,
my first image, closer
to home, the odd sense
that I am Anna too,
awash in disappointment
for the future.

ii.

> At fourteen,
through Constance Garnett –
another grim Brit – we
met for the first time.
"Sublime" said my Modern
Library jacket, or so I
remember. March, snow.
Piles and piles of it, like
Moscow, St. Petersburg.
Snow to shovel before
Father came home from work,
snow that took me away
from Anna yet back to her.
I had already convinced
myself that my family

were the Karamazovs,
and now Anna snuck into
my mind. Not unwelcomed;
true enough. People
are like that, staking
claims without invitation.
Yet Anna, dear tentative
Anna, really had no place
to go. Perhaps I'd called her
to me while conjuring the next
right book. Faith's a mystery.
With her tweed skating
outfit, her confusion,
and shame, Anna remained.

iii.

                    Every happy family's alike:
births and deaths. And every
Levin and Kitty know
to avoid cyclones, wasp
nests, lovers with wry smiles
and tales of abandonment.
Count Vronsky, part cyclone,
part wasp nest – the train wreck
about to happen, the test of
love that, once sighted, can't
be ignored. Failing to love
him, would Anna fail herself?
Put your hand in the wasp nest.
Lie on the track. At fourteen,
this seems sensible advice.

iv.

                    Forty years pass
to another late snow,
pile on pile of nuisance.
Father's now dead but
a walk should be cleared for
the dog. This time Anna comes
through Pevear/Volokhonsky,
guardians of the Karamazovs'
grief. What was learned in
forty years? Dangerous notion.
My head swims with Sinatra
singing the wee small
hours of the morning,
love that spins, burns,
disappoints. Maybe that's
what it's for. Just out
of love, smarting, I stare
at this new *Anna*'s jacket:
a black-and-white bouquet
of violets atop some bare
female knees. Nothing like
that in the book I remember.
Did she wear the scent of
Parma violets? No, that was
the Duchess of Sanseverina,
also troubled by men in
another recent translation –
a point for middle age and
re-reading "the classics".
Did Anna love blinis,
chilled vodka, caviar?
Or ever cook a meal?
Until now, I never thought
to ask.

v.

        Anna waltzes,
sups late on oysters and
champagne, follows lush,
petty Vronsky, gallops
in the vortex beside him.
I am lost: still Anna.
The train-tracks await us
yet, knowing this, I
gallop along too. No
barrier here, just the
speed our hearts can take.
When my phone rings,
it's not your voice.
Be useful, I think. Wash
the bed sheets.

vi.

        In the basement
I remember you've never
read *Anna*. Had you called,
I'd say that in one of his
lectures, Nabokov claimed
he'd read it at six, but Véra,
his wife, by three: information
more pointless than love.
Can anyone stop a train?

vii.

                    Returning
from the laundry, I
re-open *Anna* again.
"This machine is out
of order," the sign read.
My life's out of order,
too. Palm against palm,
we should have held on.
Your left, my right,
your right, my left.
"I fall in love too
easily," sings Sinatra,
as the dog snores. A
common problem *Anna*
warns against. I still
believe we can learn
from books. I have to.
But Anna and I need
a little Sinatra for
balance. That's all
I want to tell you now.

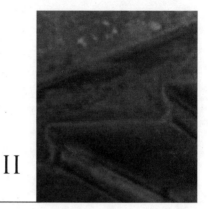

II

"Don't go to Paris. It has too many eyes. Come with me. I know a place where they are hospitable – and discreet."

– G.B. Pabst, *Pandora's Box*

OF COURSE

No one wants old men,
not even each other.
Bald spots, slack fat,
these aren't the worst
of it. Old dreams, yes,
now here we begin.

At thirty, I wanted X.
      At forty, Y.
           At fifty, Z.

With no more letters,
wanting betrays me.
But still – write it –
I'd want you. If only
I knew who you are.

FOR THE MARSCHALLIN

I will not sigh *"Ja, ja,"*
old girl, nor,

pray, blue-angel
someone young and strong

but if I do

let wonders come to
me before *"Ja, ja."*

THE GARDEN

Catalyst, terrorist,
love's counterfeit:
whichever applies,
weeds sprout from
your body to mine.

BIRDING

Crouched low, without
binoculars, I linger over
the bend in your arm –
your shoulder – neck –
your body cooing wrens
and mourning doves.

THE NEST

Like making a nest
of cobwebs and twigs –
no cosmetic appeal –
and a forgotten patch
of cloth (yellow), old
leaves, gum wrappers,
string, loving you
is less than loving,
without cloth, or leaf.
Let me take your pulse.

MUTANT TULIP

Stem and leaf merge
like Siamese twins
or partly rolled
cigarette paper, thin
edge left hanging.

One petal grows into
the leaf-stem, purple
sheen of shape and
color – silk oyster –
hidden from light.

Attachment means
trouble, as you've
said. Still, I should
have saved that bulb
for another spring.

GEORGE HERBERT'S
GLASS OF BLESSINGS

Blame the garden itself –
       assertion,
       paradox,
       myth.
This is what is – not
       high authority
       or delphic oracle –
though perhaps true
       yet cut off,
       unsuspecting.
You speak of subtle possibilities,
       like the hawthorn tree.
I say words are seldom new –
       father and son,
       mother and daughter,
       friend.

AFTER THE REVOLUTION

women adopted a style
known as *à la victime*
with butchered hair,
red silk ribbons
round their necks,
heads angled in homage
to the guillotine. Instead,
I write this for you.

DOGS ABOUT TOWN

Dogs near water
      on the rue du Chat-Qui-Pêche
Dogs with wings
      on the Cul-de-Sac de Ha! Ha!
Dogs in trouble
      on the Impasse de l'Espérance

Dogs we might walk together
      if Paris belonged to us
      and you and I to each other

Dogs, like pilgrims,
      under the table
      under the influence
      under my feet

Near perfect palindrome

THE LAST ROSE

In Paz, the guillotined penis
       spins   (*save it*)
In Frost, a strict snowy kiss
       moves on into air,
       into field   (*save it*)
In class, a pimpled blonde poet
       crosses out her best line
about the sour close of roses   (*save it*)
       but
if Stein's rose means a rose, then
       yours ought to close
       somewhere

BIRCHES

Outside the train window
white bark peels off winter
weight. What good is the book
in my lap to a man who's
not here for himself?

Of course you knew birches
on your estate at Melikhovo,
on your trip to the taiga,
in Yalta, St. Petersburg,
perhaps even a stand or two
before dying in Germany.
Their genetic composition
hasn't changed, nor their
appearance. Least sentimental
of Russians, you never preached
salvation through nature.

Still, a live tree means
soil, sun, air. It thrives
on light and water –
and you need none of
these now. But your Masha,
Trigorin, and that sad
old cab driver, yearn
for Moscow or youth
or a beloved dead child.
I can only assume
that you are past longing.

On this cold March morning
the birches sway, snow
heavy. My train pulls
out of a small station

on the way to Ottawa –
provincial towns like this
alive in your stories, places
no one could long for – and
I refuse to write that
I see the trees for
you as well. I see
them only for myself.

III

THE RETURN

For Nora Shulman

i.

The faun, Pandora, lived
alone in a flute. "Never
dismiss old legends,"
she was fond of saying.
Debussy, Ravel, a few
others, tried to coax
her out for good,
but she knew enough
to stay put: a good home
should never be taken
for granted.

ii.

           Mythology?
Pandora avoided simple
explanations. She was
in her heart a rich
key – B minor, say –
with no taste for self-
destruction. Living in
flutes can make a faun
cautious. "Music needs
chance," she told herself
on days when distractions
were lacking. A faun's
knowledge of antiquity
might get her in trouble.

The sound of old Greek
chants, winged creatures
rising, a cloud passing
by, these drew Pandora's
attention, made her wait
for Ravel or Debussy,
music a chess game that
turned her inward at least
for the morning.

iii.

But chess games are
hoaxes, love potions,
lame pastimes. Pandora's
hands felt cold when
she touched the notes,
she could have sworn
the scent of silver polish
would choke her, but
again, as the legend goes,
she had to wait. Ravel
and Debussy would
call her back, had no
choice; and she, too,
could only follow,
B minor is like that,
rich but compliant.
So legends lack choices.
She might long to be
freed of the flute, silver
polish, soft cushion –
this was her dream –
but dreams seldom
help prisoners.

iv.

                  If, waking,
Pandora once called
Ravel, or Debussy,
the legend might have
taken another turn. But
why long for a room
beyond this one – a cave,
a fjord, a suburban yard
with artificial fountain
and green plastic hose –
when she contained all
of them in her heart?
The flute is a vein, she
told herself. Be merciful.

v.

                  But beware!
She has already missed
much of her life: sweet
meals, bold embraces.
Never seen a bull fight or
heard the cry of flamenco
in the dark hole of morning.
Never, even, walked the
mountain trails of Capri.
She thought of such things
and feared for herself.

vi.

            If Debussy
had bought her a dog,
or Ravel, a cat, well, then
she might have broken
the record for loneliness.
Fauns, remember, breathe
fire, flaming to their
own rules and traditions.
With little to celebrate,
few rituals of solace or
duration. Smoke, to them,
doesn't always mean
fire. Candlelight, perhaps.
Or oil lamps – even matches.
Smoke deceives, and
Pandora has no patience
for it.

vii.

            Better not to
move, not to breathe.
Better, yet, to imagine
herself on a tall stone
column overlooking the desert.
With the moon as her lamp
she could live in the present,
forget waking sleep.
Forget Ravel and Debussy.
When moonlight kissed her
she looked at her hands,
her feet, as if she had
always loved them, known
they belonged to her

before she'd met them.
She had no idea that life
could be so simple.

viii.

            Fauns live
alone, know doubt, and
watch day drift into
week, week to month.
They carry the knowledge
on a pillow before them.
As she might say, laws
proscribed it. Even
the dream of a marriage
forbidden. Of this she
was certain. Then who needs
surprises? Adiós, dear
husband. The coup de grâce.
Anyone could see that!

ix.

She licked her wrist,
as if to take her pulse.
She knew she could
not die. Ivy grew on
the walls of her room,
eager for another inch
or two. She listened,
of course. The oil lamp
flickered, a sound like
a bull fight. The next
note, a bull's ear, if
she chose to receive it.

Who wouldn't? A bull can
mean magic without
wanting to die. If it paws,
circles, Pandora won't
turn away, the hyacinth scent
of blood, like metal polish,
can never gorge a faun,
even if it would taste like
the sweat on her wrist.

x.

She must confess to
someone – someone should
hear. Adiós, husband.
It's already too late.
The dog's died, the cat,
too. She couldn't marry
them either. She might ask
Ravel for a telescope,
he can manage that
surely – no law against
it, whatever he claims.
She feels safe in her room.
There's nothing more
to believe. She is still
alive, isn't she? With
no one to thank.
Becalmed, on her cushion,
Pandora watches the oil lamp
flicker, leans forward
and opens her lips.

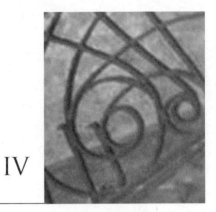

IV

"I remember my childhood but I remember the movies better."

– Joe LeSueur

THIS MORNING

If you notice
the elastic resistance of grass,
or late butterflies chasing
each other above the phlox –
from May Sarton, on Péguy –
then August's end makes sense
as a moment of invincible
fall. A season's reason has
to stay secret or hearts
might break. For now, have
raspberry jam on toast,
and Starbuck's espresso, with
no plans for the day. Since
the dog wants a share of
bread and morning, ignore
light's transition. But
remember: afternoon is
a fast horse, with eyes
like Garbo's.

THE GERMAN BREAKFAST

For Teresa Stratas

You arrange a platter of salami
    and liverwurst, thin slices of rye
        bread, several kinds of cheese,
jams, a bowl of soft-boiled eggs,
    abundance that makes strong
        coffee essential, while I recall
the time Hannah Arendt visited
    Mary McCarthy who wept
        when her friend left a plate
of breakfast salami, courtesy
    from care, but for Hannah
        a knowledge too close
to the pride of Icarus as he flew near
    the sun. In south Florida, do we
        need a Bavarian feast?
Cambozola beside the chlorine
    pool fog, even surface without
        triumphalist breakers
to catch an eye? Hawks soar
    overhead, glimpsed through
        the screened-in lanai, which
keeps the pool a polished mirror. (True, one
    copperhead discovered the hot-tub,
        but we won't speak
of it now.) White oleander – whiter
    than clouds – rustle in tentative
        breeze. You've lived in Frankfurt,
sung there *and* there *and* there, but here
    you weed as if life demands it –
        with luscious supply – while

THE RECITAL

Two men cough in a Sofia
concert hall one February
night in 1958. Then another.
                  And another.
Nearby several women feel
a feather in their throats,
swallow a choke, unwrap
                  hard candies
or hope (Bulgarian?)
and join the cacophony.
Meanwhile technicians tape
                  a legendary flight,
as it will be known: Soviet
pianist Sviatoslov Richter
making "Pictures at an Exhibition"
                  his own. Today,
on this new digital transfer,
the hackers honk clearer than
ever. Are most now dead,
                  leaving spasms
preserved for forty-four years
and timed, you'd think, to mark
the end of each phrase, every
                  ten seconds or so?
Perhaps music does this, begging
participation – fortissimo passages
bring louder coughs, imitation
                  as flattery. And
yet I feel no urge
to blow my nose. How
smooth a poem is, lacking
                  background crackle.

A GERMAN BREAKFAST

For Teresa Stratas

You arrange a platter of salami
        and liverwurst, thin slices of rye
                bread, several kinds of cheese,
jams, a bowl of soft-boiled eggs,
        abundance that makes strong
                coffee essential, while I recall
the time Hannah Arendt visited
        Mary McCarthy who wept
                when her friend left a plate
of breakfast salami, courtesy
        from care, but for Hannah
                a knowledge too close
to the pride of Icarus as he flew near
        the sun. In south Florida, do we
                need a Bavarian feast?
Cambozola beside the chlorine
        pool fog, even surface without
                triumphalist breakers
to catch an eye? Hawks soar
        overhead, glimpsed through
                the screened-in lanai, which
keeps the pool a polished mirror. (True, one
        copperhead discovered the hot-tub,
                but we won't speak
of it now.) White oleander – whiter
        than clouds – rustle in tentative
                breeze. You've lived in Frankfurt,
sung there *and* there *and* there, but here
        you weed as if life demands it –
                with luscious supply – while

Spanish moss and gardenias gone wild
        encroach on the drive, the house,
                this morning. You
offer butter, look for salt, and beyond
        knowing, inhabit so many ways
                to float a note, or shape
a line, that I'd say I'm indebted
        if there was space for words
                beside the cheese.

FOR SIMONE WEIL

Consider the childhood of John
      the Baptist. Before destiny's
water, he must have loved a pet

lamb or dove. If, like yours,
      his mother could raise only
exceptional children (barring toys,

dolls and games from the house),
      then tricks with water may have
been John's big thrill. Years later,

when you wrote that we should
      look at beauty but never
eat it, you may have forgotten

the cleansing nature of water –
      hot, cold, sacramental.
Remember the patterns of waves

under moonlight, the morning
      surf, an afternoon dip (beach,
hotel pool, no matter). As boys

John and Jesus might have river
      dunked you so often that water
would be your element, not air,

and your problem with baptism never
      arisen in letter after letter.
If we mustn't eat beauty can

we at least drink it? Even
        with Gregorian chants in
the background, renunciation tempts

death. (Like you, I love plainsong,
        and own a dozen CDs.) We
breathe beauty from air in order

to live. Life wills beauty –
        that difficult word – to be
unsettling: harsh challenge.

Without baptism, there is only
        the cross, which may be why
you envied the crucifixion.

HURRICANE

Do not look for consolation.
There is a picture: "Hart Crane
on his roof in Brooklyn,
probably in the late fall of 1928"
reads the caption, a man to hold
in your arms like Cleopatra's asp.

Do not look for redemption.
On the beach, a young father
chases his son by the shore,
they skip rocks in the waves,
sun burns their shoulders,
a day passes without mercy.

FATHER'S BEDSIDE

Three-thirty a.m. –
your hands still warm, and folded
in Calvinist manner. We say an Our Father,
Mother beyond tears. I touch your
cheek, then forehead. It's true, you
appear to be sleeping, even, as they say,
peacefully, sleeping as I've seen you
so many times on the sofa, before the TV.
We wait for the undertaker. Mother
mustn't watch them cart you away,
sixty-odd years ending like that.
I suggest leaving, she, another prayer.
You were never a man to mind
much, or take offense; just nod off.
Now a few minutes pass in silence.
Outside it's snowing, a rough end
to January. You've died just shy
of your day, the fabled ground hog's
appearance. No prayer can change
this: tonight you aren't with us.
You didn't teach in words, and
words are my air. Even here I want
to cut through the quiet. I touch
your hand again – imperceptibly cooler.
Mother fidgets with gloves and we turn
to leave, our turns next. I offer to stop
for coffee and donuts. She agrees,
a surprise: no sleep tonight. But
as we drive home, nothing is open.

MOTHER'S GARDEN

            This morning
I planted two day lilies, scab
red, rich with rust; pinks;
pink geraniums; nicotiana,
whitish pink, as if the blooms
had brushed against my
thigh and taken up
the color of flesh; several
pots of snapdragons (again,
pink); a bed of cosmos;
three Bell peppers (come
September, to be stuffed with
ground beef and rice) and in
the process replanted balsam,
violets, even columbine that
had gone their own way,
smashing into the roses – her
precious roses – and making
a nuisance of themselves. Not
my choices, exactly, but
the best of two nurseries and
Home Depot. Hardy annuals,
garden ready. And like all
gardens, this one's planted
with time. Of course I felt
the present turning to past,
engulfing loss (plants do that)
while my mind's eye saw
thick beds of impatiens
in Beverly Hills, clumps of
oriental poppies and lavender

iris in Santa Fe, the white
garden at Sissinghurst, and
wondered if I'll make it to
eighty-one, as she has,
still ready for weeding.

LULU AND CHICHI

"Like a couple of monkeys," Grandpa used to say about
    the nicknames Mary Lou and I gave each other
        at one and one-and-a-half.

Fifty years later, first cousins still yammer as Mary sits
    on the front porch of a swank nursing home
        where we visit Aunt Rudie, now ninety-three.

"All here, except the dead ones," she quips. Mother blinks,
    perhaps lost in tomorrow's CAT scan, or
        the late August light in the willows.

A horse and buggy clomp by. This is Amish country,
    northeastern Ohio, and later we'll pick corn
        from a roadside stand.

Shell-shocked Lulu, whose husband sought
    internet loving, sighs deeply. The wattage from
        too many electro-shock treatments has,

she'll tell you, fried her brain; her thyroid's shot;
    depression's a bummer. "This is a nice
        place," she says, "I'd like to sit here

reading a Nancy Drew." Rudie smiles, uncertain
    of what she hears, and my mother, a youngster
        at eighty-one, takes her hand.

How far back these women go – decade on decade
    to the early twenties, when their mothers,
        sisters Rozsa and Mari in summer lace blouses

(one of those yellowing in a trunk in Mother's basement)
 watched as young Rose – nickname Rudie hadn't stuck yet –
 rocked her new cousin, born on the feast day

of Mary Magdalen that hot July after the end of the first
 world war. We won't speak of the accumulation of dead
 ones, not during this visit.

Willows rustle as Rudie jiggles the leash on my dogs:
 "I'm going to get a puppy when I go home."
 Her eyes know, but can't say,

that she'll leave here only by ambulance or coffin.
 Eighty-one Julys ago it didn't cross her mind
 that her days would end in an unfamiliar bed

with a stranger for a roommate. And later, when Lulu and I
 began to shape sounds, depression and poetry never
 occurred to us, nor this death toll:

in their nineties, first Grandma, who managed an exit line –
 "So this is life, not worth much, is it?"
 Then Rozsa, in haywire, vomiting excrement;

next, their eldest daughters; husbands galore, including Rudie's
 Jules, the Chevalier double, and last year, my father;
 our count keeps mounting. No wonder

I want one bright thought. Lulu sighs again while Rudie
 and Mother watch willows weep. Next summer's time
 enough to visit that cathedral in Vézelay

where miraculous monkey business transferred
 Mary Magdalen's bones to France from Jerusalem.
 Happy ending, after all.

WALKING IN BROOKLINE

Early morning. Morgan sniffs, Zoli pulls –
      that's their way. Every ten feet
or so Morgan turns his head back,
      floppy spaniel ears tossing like
the mane of a nervous debutante,
      to make sure I'm still holding
the leash. We wait at the School Street
      cross-light, by the double-T
intersection of Cypress and Washington,
      before Brookline's fine library.
The light is silver, the trees July green.
      Taking warm air into my lungs, I
say "Stay" to Zoli, eager pug. Somewhere
      a car horn sounds like Gabriel's
trumpet. Then I notice him: awash
      in gorgeous light. Since
last fall he's been stripped of
      the mossy green patina that
made him one with spring leaves
      or overcast winter sky.
Now he's restored, this monument to
      the civil-war dead: lone soldier
on his horse, head back, bugle
      at his lips, proud bugle boy,
reminder that Brookline sons once
      answered their nation's call, went
off to duty, war and death. Someone
      like him must have been nursed
by Whitman during that long wet
      spring of 1863. My friends tell me
about the renovation – friends who've
      just sold their condo around
the corner for a 100-k-plus profit
      (we shake our heads over real

estate, naturally). After several weeks
            of scaffolding, a metal cage
for two climbers who resembled boys on
            a jungle gym, bronze was bronze
again, the bugle, brass. No sign had been
            posted, cleaning clear enough.
Then a photographer came to take the
            official portrait. Today
Morgan squats and pees, not on
            the lawn but in the middle of
the sidewalk, where the red outline
            of a heart with FUCK inside
has been chalked. Zoli pulls ahead.
            It's strange, if you notice, how
we insist on putting names to things,
            as if tags assure ownership. Pug –
carlin, mopszli – what do these words say
            about my flat-nosed friend? Or
"civil-war soldier" about bronze bugler?
            Brookline – this old town,
incorporated in 1703 – is nothing to me,
            nothing, now that my friends plan
to leave, and the statue of all men
            at war, hell, it's less and more
than all the boys it stands for.
            Hundreds of years from now
the sorry creature may be buried deep
            under Brookline, and a few people
digging for treasure will unearth
            him and wonder who he meant
to welcome. What kind of place
            have we come to, they'll ask,
not knowing that I stood here once
            with the same question.
What else can we do? We walk.
            Walk on.

TORCH SONG

"Human life is *impossible*. But it is only affliction which makes
us feel this." – Simone Weil

Mark is making brownies,
Larry, on his second scotch, reads
someone's fresh memoirs, bored
Morgan snores at my feet and
Andrea Marcovicci sings, full-
throated: *"When a lovely flame dies..."*

After four months beside me,
sleeping through poetry classes
or under my desk, time came
to take Morgan home to Echo Park,
absurdly named – for what? –
no one here can tell me.

Love and loss and longing,
over and over, change key
but keep minor tonality, these CD
songs are fine to slit your wrists
by, the weight of waiting
replaced by memory's burdens:

so much to not forget. Smoke
won't get in our eyes (no one
ever lights up) but we wonder
why the night leaves us chilled
by unease. Behind Mark,
pink-flamingo Christmas lights

hang aglow in a bare kitchen
window. The camellia I planted
earlier today, how will it fare
this first night in new soil,
spreading out roots to rain
and filtered light?

Vintage ornaments, reports
the *Times*, set record eBay highs,
along with teddy bears recycled
from mink coats. "Morgan," I say
to the dog, "You'll be fine here.
You know you'll be fine." Still,

he climbs into my lap, stares up
beseechingly, as if the ways of
humans will always puzzle him.
"When a lovely flame dies..."
How many men and women have
torched those fearful words –

with tears, with rue – which fill
the livingroom while the dog
rests his head on my chest and
sighs? "Listen to this," Mark
calls, then reads from a pamphlet
that chocolate can increase good

cholesterol, and decrease
bad, or so researchers now
think. Just half an ounce
each day. But poison, of course,
to dogs – loss always ready
to get you, if you forget it.

Ahead a new song hoard of
Peggy Lee. Drinks flow,
as in any ceremonial hall
after battle. Yet despite e-mail
and satellite, no newscast notes
the street dogs of Kabul or Kandahar.

FOR ZOLI

"Dog" and "cancer" as words
in a line may be too
much for a poem
to bear – poems have needs
that differ from poets',
hate what some will call
sentiment, an excess of life
that you, my friend, now
face in another form.
Add "chemo", add "death",
and the eye turns away –
where's room for irony?
But you are a clown
at heart, breathing deeper
than any poem can.

LEGACY

Named after country manors
      or ancestral seats,
the nursing homes give gentle
      yet firm guidance,
like private schools for teens
      who've run amok.
What's the difference between
      the adolescent and senile
brain? "She's confused but pliable,"
      head nurse Debbie says
as if to reassure, and I tell myself
      with my right lobe (or left?)
that anyone in trouble would be lucky
      to find refuge here, while
my left lobe (or right?) says, "Start
      stockpiling Seconals."
Nearby, my young mother in
      fake emerald earrings
carries a holiday platter lovingly.
      "What did you always make
for Christmas?" I ask the old one,
      and she replies, "Chicken?"
"Think bigger," I prod, and
      with that new, tentative
smile, she offers, "Ham?"
      But that meant Easter, yet
a nod seems right. Papered in
      the best house-and-home
style – sweet floral pastels –
      the walls a solid fortress
against dementia, with a locked
      ward just in case,
Mother's new room (room, not yet
      home) beckons monastically.

(Protestant church services on
            Sunday afternoon, Mass on
Tuesdays, before handicrafts.)
            My old woman doesn't
recognize her own recliner until
            she sits down and stares
out the window, frowning
            at a snowy parking lot.
"You can watch the world go by,"
            I suggest – something
has to be said – at once regretting
            idiocy, yet Mother agrees,
"It's good to see people." She doesn't
            appear to notice that someone's
left behind a pot of death-defying silk
            tulips, the palest brain pink.
Will she join in games of Bingo
            and Uno and Hearts?
(Yes, yes and yes.) She is once
            again a fifteen-year-old
card-playing fool, cross-legged
            on the bed with her sister,
long dead, beside other drooping heads
            that call for their goners in
the middle of the night. Oh, Seconals
            anyone? Be calm, I warn
myself: Luis will paint her nails, she
            can have her hair done weekly,
the food's better than fine. But this is
            my young woman wearing
fake emeralds, to be loved now
            in ways still unknown.

LARKIN WAS HALF-RIGHT

After that four a.m. pee, you
never think of youthful erections
or porno alerts heading southward,
but of strong young bladders
able to hold sleep longer
than two hours, until that six a.m.
pee, which Larkin forgot.
In those dull restless minutes
there's decades to recall
lost bodies, but from my window
the moon's movement feels less pressing,
and the old pastoral's merely one story,
since those shepherds sometimes turned
to each other, not just to Phoebe
or Clarissa or Chlorene, while the moon
refused to look away. Raleigh was almost
right, too – after a certain age
you can't live alone in the country,
the moon keeps repeating itself
without much practical help.
Tonight, over my balcony (forget
Romeo and Cyrano) nothing
climbs or shines, no sad steps
beckon. My burden's my bladder –
skip the pain of being young.
I won't open my curtain, I've seen
the moon before, known its pull;
no. And the dark moon above
doesn't care about touching, in love
with its pattern, its familiar old route.
Yet there's something to learn from
such repetition, if only counting
bodies could return you to sleep.

FOLLOWING GARBO

"Dead?" she once remarked,
"I have been dead for many years."
Moving her plastic trolls around
under the sofa, a diet of yoghurt
and wheat bread, some vodka,
long walks, early evenings with
"Wheel of Fortune" on the bedroom TV
and her old movies, rarely. I've got
to die too, leaving books and shoes,
untouched cheese, stale crackers.
She liked to call herself "a little
old man" – learn from that smile.

V

A PUNCTURE TO THE HEART

(September 10, 1898 and February 19, 2001)

i. *The wound*

Wounds are silent. They may
weep, but without sound.
>One day you stop,
>and I'm not consulted
>about the hour –
>*will stop,* actually –
>yet that verb seems
>harder to write.
The wound becomes the heart.

ii. *The question*

It began with a question: Is
the artery blocked? Common
enough, asked all the time,
though not, before, to me.
Add to this one assassin
in the making: Luigi Luccheni,
and one sitting duck:
Elizabeth of the Dual Monarchy.
Then, also, the thought of no
beloved face in particular.

Is a puncture to the heart
like an electric shock?
Like sudden love, or
death? Fear of fears, yes.

iii. *Elizabeth Amelia Eugenia*

She offers distraction, the official
place to send black thoughts,
like an employees' suggestion
box that's seldom opened.

The young are skittish, closed
off to illness other than
their own. Dead empresses
can use attention too.

Without warning, or pre-
testing, she dressed for travel,
perhaps thinking of Franz
Josef back in Vienna.

Or her dead son Rudolf,
who shot himself and
his mistress at Mayerling,
that borrowed hunting lodge.

I see her in the guise of
Ava Gardner playing E.
in a '69 turkey, ripe
plum of a queen.

iv. *Pre-testing: x-rays*

In this small cubicle,
putting on a thin faded gown,
I look at naked knees,
ashamed to be sitting in
a cramped closure that belongs
to the Grimm Brothers, corner
for punishment or time out

to humble body and spirit.
Too late for transformation
now, just pay-up time.

v. *Numbing-out*

After Rudolf's death, you wandered
incognito: Biarritz, San Remo,
Lausanne. "I want to die alone,"
you cautioned a lady-in-waiting.
You preferred the sea, you walked
beside it for hours, compliant
as the shoreline. No need to hurry,
no one spoke to you there. So
many ways to be numbed out.
A nurse offers me my choice
of sedatives: "It helps you relax."
But why would I want to do that?

vi. *The puncture site*

My puncture occurs beside
     the frozen groin – left
     or right – depending
on how the doc is handed
     (this I learn later, from
     an emergency-room
     resident who can't tell
     the difference between
     an aneurysm and hematoma)
and then a scope's inserted
     with a flick of the wrist
     as quick as a pirouette,
my body the stage. Flat on my back,
     hands under my head,

elbows out, I am unlike E.,
who met her puncture while
standing on the quay,
awaiting a steamer.

vii. *The procedure*

Like cellophane-bagged wings, which
remind me of dry-cleaning
wraps aflap in the wind,
two metal arms shift, flutter,
as if ready to take off or
at least split this operating
theater, as it's called, translucent
butterflies moving over
a place they haven't
seen before. Why cellophane?
I never learn. My groin's
frozen, the scope inserted,
the TV monitor turned on to a
silver blue screen that
shows the thin wire moving
towards my heart, a pewter line
as graceful as the unfolding
root of a rare plant in some
"Nature" documentary for PBS, only
I'm the forest floor, ocean
ridge, moonscape. I
try to connect the shadow image
to my veins, chest, lungs –
are those my lungs? – pale
metallic lakes bypassed by that
determined scope ready to give
my heart a shot of dye that
heats from ass outward, a warm
buzz spreading like an oil slick

of pleasure – "If you could turn
that into a pill, you'd make a fortune
        on the street," I say, and Doctor
        cracks a smile while reminding me
to breathe evenly – or not breathe, just
        then, I can't recall which – so I
        fall silent as we near the end.
His promise – no pain – proves true
        enough, and I wonder
        if E. mistook her assassin's
thin blade for a pin-prick,
        a tick, a bug bite, or just another
        twitch that proves middle age will
have its way. Think: she walked to
        her stateroom, collapsed, and
        a spot of blood spread across
her chemise. No time to panic – no certainty
        that a butterfly machine would lift
        its arms to set her free.
She did not wait for test results,
        she waited to die, Luccheni's
        name unknown to her.

viii. *Post operative*

"No blockage."

No physical problem
        explains my chest
        pains. *No blockage*:
it has to sink in.
        A case of heartache
        without consequences.
"The heart of a young man,"
        says Doctor. We have
        to laugh: what else?

ix. *Post angiogram information*

It's okay to climb a few
       stairs, if necessary,
to resume driving
       in twenty-four hours
and "sexual activities"
       (as the brochure said)
       in forty-eight, but
avoid lifting heavy objects
       for one week
(alas, lifting a lover must
       be forbidden)
as well as regular exercise
       for three to four days,
and showers only – no baths! –
       for safety's sake.
If the puncture site
       starts to bleed,
call for help: never
       drive yourself anywhere.
And don't plan air travel with-
       out asking your cardiologist.

None of the above, of course,
       applied to the Kaiserin.

x. *The autopsy*

Not long before Luccheni
struck E's chest, a spa doctor
wanted to X-ray the royal
heart. "I will not," she said,
"be dissected while I'm alive."
Her wound, v-shaped, sat
fourteen centimeters below

the left collarbone, and four
above the nipple of her left
breast, the file's entry point
to eighty-five millimeters of
                    her heart.

xi. *The body in question*

Perhaps I'd secretly hoped
that, like a prizefighter,
someone would clench
hands over my head. I won't
tell about hematomas,
aneurysms, all bother.
Or about doctors missing
the point, the clot,
the vein. Instead, I've
put down everything
I know: a pretty face
still wounds me, and
a puncture to the heart
may have its uses.

VI

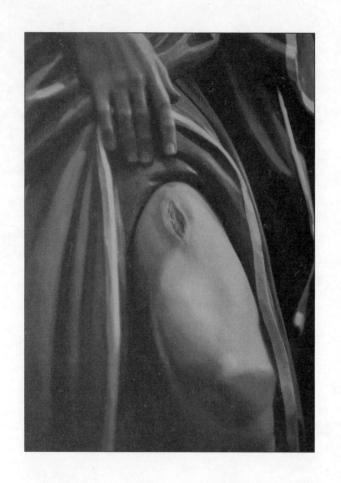

THE HERMIT'S KISS

Touch me. My wound is for your hands. If you prefer to pray, remember that I cannot hear. Listen to me instead. They thought I emanated a sense of death. How can I know? I spoke reluctantly.

One historian – his name does not matter, for he, too, will die – wrote that "Mongol movements across previously isolating distances in all probability brought the bacillus *Pasteurella pestis* to the rodents of the Eurasian steppe for the first time." And from there, to Europe. To Piacenza. In northern Italy.

This search for causes, sources, origins, has never interested me.

My life is the history of plague. My body, my shell, is made of plaster and wood. Bones, flesh, blood – they felt the same. The carver had a name: Eugenio. He loved dogs, the scent of baking bread, mushroom risotto and young men with strong arms. Which may explain why his knife and hands formed the mass that became this body with such patience. Ignoring my pain, he gave me health and beauty. Did he dare whisper my name as an endearment? It was eighty, ninety years ago, no matter – a short time to me – and anyway, I probably forgave him.

My bones, of wood, were covered with plaster in order to absorb color: *indigo, cremisi d'Alizarine, terra di Siena bruciata.* I can't recall the painter's name, if I ever knew it. I believe he preferred the dog to me, just another man in robes. Dogs were rare, he didn't get one every day, the sentimentalist. So my cheeks are too flushed and high-colored, more like the heroine's in a romance than a feverish man's; my lips – a sweet bow – could leave their print on yours.

On Sunday mornings children always notice me. I am the saint with the dog. The dog who carried a bread roll in its mouth.

Even as a child I preferred solitude to the company of my family. I liked to walk in the hillsides of Montpellier. The scent of thyme and rosemary still clings to me. I never missed great rooms, fine tapestries – my life was not to be wasted.

My people, wealthy merchants, lived as aristocrats might. They valued safety and comfort. Mother often kept a bowl of rose water in her chambers; she liked to stay in bed all morning, even into the afternoon. I believe she was praying.

As I grew older, I remained in the hills overnight. Eventually people frowned, as if I were fanatic, yearning to be part of the family of saints; even then, the world had no place for me. But I knew the wisdom of refusing all temptations. The flesh is not easily exhausted. I would pray for an hour or so before going to sleep. At night I liked to watch the stars.

Hermit, pilgrim: only words.

Across the street, this Corso Italia on another continent, peacocks shop for Versace sweaters, couples drink *latte macchiato*. It is the Christmas season when fresh snow fills the trees and gentle plump women buy the imported sweet bread called *panettone* in its bright blue boxed stamped "Motta" in gold. "The original Milanese recipe," proclaims the box, but I wouldn't know about that; I never saw an orange, much less candied peel. Such delicacies you have at your finger tips! No one visits me on this cold Saturday afternoon.

So the truth appears in details, you say? Are details facts? I leave that issue to others. In 1346, several years before I was born, the bubonic infection returned to Europe. (I died from it at the age of thirty.) This was the plague's second appearance, now as the Black Death. According to historians, the last previous mention of the plague by Christian writers dates from 767. Almost four hundred years after *Pasteurella pestis* found a home, its ecological niche, as you call it, in the burrows of the black rat, whose fleas carried the plague. Rat; flea; man, woman, child. Flea bites, at first, then by human contact – touch me! – and through the air, as you inhaled the contamination of coughing, sneezing. Soon vileness surrounded us. Our air bled with it, our bedding stank. Even the soup we ate tasted of death. No, I will not tell you how ships carried the infection across the Atlantic, or to the remote ports of Europe. We never knew, and you already know enough. There is always a plague brewing. And I am always dying of it.

At twenty, after my parents died, I sold our land and set out for Rome.

The roads left me breathless. I began to cough, with a pain deep in my chest. Many times, men could have killed me.

Outside the walls of each new town, corpses piled up. Inside, I heard rumors of witches, and of executions. Once someone gave me a piece of leathery sausage, but I tossed it to a stray dog. I could have lived on wild olives.

Often I wondered where I would die, and how. The torch-lit processions passing the lane where I slept usually meant another funeral. Bells rang continuously.

The afternoon passes as usual. A young girl visits Mary: Does she have a vocation? An elderly man dressed in black dips his fingers into holy water, makes the sign of the cross on his forehead. After looking about – perhaps for Father – he leaves, frowning.

Gradually the church darkens.

Then, out of nowhere, a woman with long graying black hair stands before me. She focuses a camera while the bearded man behind her left shoulder comments, apparently in a low voice. But I can't hear, as I said before. With one hand he gestures toward my wound. The camera tilts upward.

I believe they are speaking of light.

I am embarrassed that my leg thrusts out like a chorus girl's (I know about them – eternity isn't static). My wound glistens, its hard pink lips a wild rose, the *vagina dentate*, the Sacred Heart. It burns me, burns me.

Roch, Rocco, Rock. Try and remember.

One year, after visiting Rome, I met the plague in Piacenza where, tradition has it, I was fed in the woods by a lone dog. And I cured fellow sufferers miraculously, before returning to Montpellier, and my cruel uncle. This seems a reasonable account, if you can believe that a man dying of plague would walk from Italy to France. Why not? What you believe is of little consequence to me.

My uncle would not see me. Denied me, even. Had me imprisoned as an impostor. Could he not see? I watched him kick his horse once, a foolish man.

The making of a cave – every hermit learns now. Rule #1: Keep possessions to a minimum. Yesterday's newspapers told of a nameless old man who died under a bridge, where he apparently slept. Around his body police found his few possessions: an empty rye bottle, several foul shirts rolled into a ball, torn magazines, half a dozen wire hangers, a chipped mug, a bag of stale doughnuts, an unopened jar of peanut butter, three books of matches, a plastic bag stuffed with other plastic bags, all carefully concealed under another plastic bag as protection from the rats who shared his home. He understood how to make a cave.

The winters are cold in Piacenza.

A hand, dipping cloth into brandy, smells of the sweet old wine we used for cleansing. Each sore has a stench of its own. I have watched hands move around the wounds, over and over, pity in the touch. Whose hands were they? Mine? I have seen too many wounds, yet what I wanted most was another.

Several days after the flea bite: swelling glands, headache, nausea, vomiting, bloody diarrhea, blotchy red skin rash. Then the first bubo appears, one to four inches in diameter, in the groin, or the arm pit, or beside the neck. But usually in the groin. Tender, at first, it fills with yellowish liquid, a mixture of puss and blood. Now chills, fever, rapid pulse, even delirium. If death doesn't occur, your infection might spread to the lungs, which develop abscesses. Death by pneumonia. Or – for there always seems to be an or – the buboes might be infected by other bacteria. But I won't elaborate. These are the things you become. God's tokens, some called them, the buboes. Or, simply, tokens.

Some say I died back in Montpellier, others cite Lombardy. Relics were claimed across Europe, from Arles to Venice. Look me up in any dictionary of saints, under Roch – you'll see. A cult emerged, and I became patron of the plague-stricken.

And then the Black Death died down, taking with it a third of the population of Europe. Two hundred years later, people no longer needed me, although revivals have happened. Outbreaks of cholera in the nineteenth century found me again. Remember, I am always waiting.

And the dog? Of course there is no truth to the story of the dog. Is that what you want to hear? You want me to say that he belongs to legend, to fancy? You would be wrong. There were always a pack of dogs barking furiously.

You do not understand miracle. No – I said miracle, in the singular. Miracle is a place. You can live there, if you like. I once lived in miracle: that is the nature of prayer.

The man and woman prepare to leave. After taking one more picture, of him at my feet, she puts her camera into a leather bag, then buttons her coat; he pulls on gloves. They look about the empty church and nod to each other.

Darkness quickens my memory. I will myself to forget.

Thyme, sage, rosemary.

Across the street, rats come out to play in narrow lanes behind the vegetable stores, restaurants.

Stay with me tonight, for one whole, single night, as if it could go from sleep to death.

ALONE, WITH A BOOK,
AT THE END OF THE WORLD

Instead of fire or ice,
CNN will go blank,
no one to count bodies.
So little to know left,
so little to see now,
just unnamed colors
before my eyes, spinning
past the edge of sight.
So little to cry for, hearts
filled with war despite
the books we claim to love,
the books we've defiled.
No point in giving its title
here, all books being one.

BRASSAÏ IN BERLIN, 1921

The foggy autumn turned rainy
on October 23rd – twenty-five years
to the day before I was born – wrote
young Gyula Halász to his parents.

Remember, they said, a sound
current holds all creation together.
Feed stray birds in September;
light strong lamps if you must.
The obvious deduction is wrong.

LATE AUTUMN

Putting down words changes
      nothing of woe – green
thought – emotion's motion
      wants to move beyond
meaning not its own.
      There is no house.
There is neither husband
      nor wife. Whatever
we have now cannot last.

DRINKING SONG

Far away, across
a celadon sea, you
raise your face to
the moon. I'm no
longer waiting, am I?

NOTES AND ACKNOWLEDGEMENTS

Many thanks are due my editors at Fitzhenry & Whiteside, to Evan Jones for his thoughtful readings and generous suggestions, and to Richard Dionne, who saw the book through publication. Thanks as well to Barry Callaghan, Chris Doda, Mardel and Marc Sanzotta, Teresa Stratas, Rosemary Sullivan, Penelope Tzougros and Priscila Uppal for reading poems in manuscript.

I also want to note several books that were helpful: *Paris in the Fifties* by Stanley Karnow (New York: Times Books/Random House, 1997); *Elizabeth, Empress of Austria* by Egon Corti, translated by Catherine Alison Phillips (New Haven: Yale University Press, 1936); and *Plagues and Peoples* by William H. McNeill (New York: Anchor Press/Doubleday, 1976). Epigraphs come from *The Adventures of Sindbad* by Gyula Krúdy, translated by George Szirtes (Budapest: Central European University Press, 1998); G. W. Pabst's *Pandora's Box* (Home Vision Cinema); and Joe LeSueur's *Digressions on Some Poems by Frank O'Hara: A Memoir* (New York: Farrar, Straus and Giroux, 2003).

The photograph on page 76, before "The Hermit's Kiss", is reproduced courtesy of Gail Geltner. The statue of St. Roch is located in St. Clare's Roman Catholic Church on St. Clair Avenue West, in Toronto.

"Brassaï in Berlin, 1921" also uses the Hungarian photographer's birth name, Gyula Halász (1899-1984).

And, finally, special thanks to the journals that originally published some of the work in this collection:

Antigonish Review – "Alone, with a Book, at the End of the World", "Drinking Song"
Cimarron Review – "Lulu and Chichi", "The Recital" and "This Morning"
Descant – "Re-reading *Anna Karenina*"
Exile – "A Puncture to the Heart", "For Zoli" and "The Hermit's Kiss"
Malahat Review – "Birches"
Variety Crossing – "Alone, with a Book, at the End of the World", "Drinking Song" and "The Nest" (translated into Korean)
Worcester Review – "For Simone Weil"

ABOUT THE AUTHOR

RICHARD TELEKY is the author of *The Paris Years of Rosie Kamin*, which received the Ribalow Prize for the best novel of 1999, *Pack Up the Moon* (2001), *Goodnight, Sweetheart and Other Stories* (1993), *Hungarian Rhapsodies: Essays on Ethnicity, Identity and Culture* (1997), and most recently, *Winter in Hollywood* (2006). He teaches at York University, Toronto. This is his debut collection of poetry.